Zookeeper

Steven Otfinoski

Cavendish Square
New York

Published in 2014 by Cavendish Square Publishing, LLC
303 Park Avenue South, Suite 1247, New York, NY 10010

Library of Congress Cataloging-in-Publication Data
Otfinoski, Steven.
Zookeeper / by Steven Otfinoski.
p. cm. — (Careers with animals)
Includes index.
ISBN 978-1-62712-473-7 (hardcover) ISBN 978-1-62712-474-4 (paperback) ISBN 978-1-62712-475-1 (ebook)
1. Zoo keepers — Juvenile literature. 2. Zoos — Vocational guidance — Juvenile literature. I. Otfinoski, Steven. II. Title.
QL50.5 O84 2014
636.08—dc23

Editorial Director: Dean Miller
Senior Editor: Peter Mavrikis
Copy Editor: Fran Hatton
Art Director: Jeffrey Talbot
Designer: Amy Greenan
Photo Researcher: Julie Alissi, J8 Media
Production Manager: Jennifer Ryder-Talbot
Production Editor: Andrew Coddington

CONTENTS

ONE

A Passion for Animals

It's early morning at the Pittsburgh Zoo in Pennsylvania, and Willie Theison is going out for his daily run. Only Willie's run is not your ordinary jog. His running mates are six elephants, weighing an average of nearly 9,000 pounds (over 4,000 kg). Willie is head elephant keeper at the zoo. Running is good for the elephants and helps keep them healthy. After the run down the public footpaths, Willie returns the elephants to their home, a large barn, just in time to greet the first human visitors of the day. Running with elephants is not for the fainthearted. But to Willie, they are his friends. "By hanging out with them, we make everything a pleasurable experience," he explains. About his morning runs, Willie says: "I could never give that up."

Willie Theison is totally committed to his job. Zookeepers are among the hardest working animal care professionals. Some of them work up to 50 hours each week, including nights, weekends, and holidays. Animals live in zoos 24 hours a day and someone has to be on call at all times. There is always something to do, and the unexpected can happen at any moment. Zookeepers see their work as more than just a job. It is a calling that they are passionate about.

(Opposite) An African elephant gets his head brushed by his keeper.

Bathtime for the Elephants

Elephants not only have to be exercised daily, they have to be bathed as well. At Washington's National Zoo, the elephants are bathed each morning at 8:30. The zoo has four elephants and it takes an hour to bathe all of them. "They really enjoy being bathed," says head elephant keeper Marie Galloway. "In the wild they bathe as frequently as possible."

Two of the elephants at a time are led into the bathing cage. First each is brushed down, then livestock shampoo is applied to their bodies and the skin scrubbed. Often the elephants will stick their trunks into the bucket of shampoo and drink it. "It's nontoxic soap," explains keeper Debby Flynn. "It always make me nauseous (to watch her drink it), but they love it." Finally, the elephants are rinsed down with a hose and then fed their morning breakfast of oats and bran. It doesn't take them long to get dirty again and ready for the next morning's bath.

Leslie Trenary, a senior keeper at the world-famous San Diego Zoo in California, puts it this way: "The best part of my job is the relationship I have with the animals I care for … the bond and trust that is gained through consistent patience and willingness to adapt to them. It's an honor to care for them."

Animals on Display

A zoo, short for zoological park or garden, is a place where animals are kept and put on display for people to observe. Zoos grew out of people's fascination with animals and their behavior. The first zoos

Willie Theison gently guides some of his elephants into the water at the Pittsburgh Zoo.

were not meant for the public, but for the private pleasure of kings, queens, and emperors. One of the grandest of these ancient zoos was the 1,500-acre Garden of Intelligence built in 1000 BC by the Chinese emperor Wen Wang.

The first public zoos were created by the ancient Greeks. They saw zoos as places not only to be entertained by animals, but also to study them. This is still one of the main purposes of zoos today. Small zoos called **menageries** first appeared in Europe in the Middle Ages. Sometimes only a few animals, such as bears and lions, would be displayed in cages and pits. The animals were often treated poorly and even abused. Larger and more humane public zoos were established in Vienna, Austria, in 1752 and Paris in 1793. The Vienna zoo, called the Schönbrunn, is the oldest zoo still in operation today. One of the first zoos in the United States was the Central Park Zoo in New York City, which opened in 1864. The Lincoln Park Zoo opened in Chicago 10 years later. Washington D.C.'s National Zoo opened in 1889 and remains the only zoo run by the federal government. The Philadelphia Zoo established the first Children's Zoo in 1938.

Today there are 142 **accredited** zoos in the United States that house, collectively, 6,000 different animal **species**. American zoos employ 142,000 people. Only a small number of these employees are zookeepers. Most keepers, like Willie Theison, work in a particular area or section of the zoo with one or more kinds of animals.

Royal Menagerie, Exeter Change, Strand.

In menageries, such as this one in 1820s London, animals were confined in cramped cages and often treated inhumanely.

(Above) Keeping records of animals' height and mass is part of a zookeeper's job. This keeper is measuring a giant tortoise.

(Right) This keeper doesn't seem the least concerned about the sharp quills on her friend, a porcupine.

Enrichment is an important part of a zookeeper's day.

Feeding is just one part of a zookeeper's job.

Should You Be a Zookeeper?

- Do you love caring for animals?
- Do you have the stamina, strength, and interest to work with animals on a daily basis?
- Do you have the patience to deal with problems that arise with animals?
- Do you like working with people as well as animals?
- Do you have good powers of observation?
- Do you enjoy your academic classes, particular biology, math, and English, and can you earn top grades in them?
- Are you willing to go to school for two or more years at a traditional college or one with a teaching zoo?
- Are you willing to work for several years as a volunteer with no pay or an intern for very little pay to gain experience in zoo work?

If you answered "yes" to all of these questions, zookeeper could be a good career choice for you.

Each keeper is responsible for the physical and mental health of his or her animals. The keeper feeds and cleans up after the animals and maintains the **enclosure** where they live. The keeper trains and plays with the animals and writes daily reports on their health and behavior. Another, but equally important, part of the keeper's job is to inform and educate the zoo's guests about the animals and the importance of protecting them and their natural **habitat**. Being a zookeeper is a demanding job that requires patience, thoroughness, devotion, strength, courage, and perseverance. But the people who care for the zoo's many animals wouldn't want it any other way.

Zookeeper Martin Damboldt feeds a baby sable antelope milk from a bottle at the Berlin Zoo in Germany. After the mother of the one-month-old antelope stopped feeding it, zookeepers intervened and now feed the antelope daily milk from a bottle.

TWO

The Path to Success

Fifty years ago most zookeepers had no more than a high school education. Their duties consisted of feeding and cleaning the animals and maintaining their cages or enclosures. Today, the job of zookeeper is far more sophisticated, and candidates need both a college education and extensive hands-on experience.

Many successful zookeepers discovered their passion for animals at an early age. Don Boyer, **curator** of **herpetology** at the San Diego Zoo, is a good example. "By the sixth grade I decided I wanted to be a curator of a large reptile collection," he says. Boyer collected snakes and other reptiles at home and volunteered on weekends in the reptile house at the Baltimore Zoo while in high school. Although he attended college and earned a degree, Boyer claims he got more out of his volunteer work with animals and his involvement with the Society for the Study of Amphibians and Reptiles (SSAR) and the American Zoo and Aquarium Association (AZA). After college, he was hired as a keeper at the San Antonio Zoo and later the Dallas Zoo, both in Texas, and then worked his way up to supervisor and, finally, curator. "You have to be motivated from within," Boyer says, when seeking a career in zookeeping.

(Opposite) Courses in biology and other life sciences are important for someone seeking a career as a zookeeper. The students in this photo are studying the skeleton of a monitor lizard.

Finding the Right College

While a wide range of colleges could provide you with a solid grounding in biology and other life sciences, you want to make sure the school you choose has as much to offer you in animal science and care as possible. Here are some questions to ask your academic advisors.

- How successful have graduates of this school been in getting jobs as zookeepers or other zoo positions?
- Do academic advisors take an active role in helping students plan for a career in zoo work?
- If this school doesn't have facilities where I can get hands-on experience working with animals, are there facilities nearby (zoos, nature centers, veterinarians) where I can work as a volunteer or intern?
- Are there enough courses in animal science and behavior that will provide me with the academic background I need to pursue my career as a zoo professional?
- Are there clubs, newsletters, or other activities that will allow me to meet and connect with students who share my interest in working with animals?

(Opposite) Keeper Sarah Hall helps count some of the meerkats at Bristol Zoo in England. The annual animal "census" is carried out at the start of each year and includes inventorying more than 400 species, from tiny insects, fish and birds, to seals, gorillas, and monkeys.

(Right) A college freshman works in a biology lab at Consumnes River College in Sacramento, California.

A Bachelor's Degree

If you are serious about entering the field of zoo keeping, you could go to a traditional four-year college and major in any life science subject, such as biology, **zoology**, animal science, or **ecology**. You should also take courses in math, an important skill for zoo work. You should also take English courses. Zookeepers need to have good communication skills. They need to be able to write clearly and concisely in daily logs and reports. You might also consider a course in public speaking. Keepers often have to talk to visitors and answer their questions. Some keepers give lectures on their animals and perform animal demonstrations and special programs for the public.

If you have a strong interest in one type of animal or animal group (mammals, birds, or reptiles, for instance) it would be smart to take college courses that are about them. It will better prepare you to specialize in one zoo section, although newly hired keepers often work with many different animals at first.

While classroom learning is important, you need to get hands-on experience with animals, too. Most traditional colleges won't have a zoo or animal center to work in, so you should look for nearby zoos, nature centers, or other animal care facilities where you can volunteer. As a student in animal care, you might even get an internship, but don't expect to be paid for your work. The experience, however, will be invaluable later, when you apply for zoo keeping positions. Zoos are looking to hire people who already have experience with animals and are familiar with the kinds of tasks required of them.

There are masters' programs in zoo management at some colleges, but unless you are looking to move directly into a supervisory position, you don't need a master's degree. You may not even need a bachelor's degree.

An Associate Degree

You don't have to attend a four-year college to prepare for a career in zoo work. In fact, there are some advantages to attending a two-year private or community college that has a small teaching zoo. These schools offer a more cooperative training experience, combining daily work in a zoo with classroom work. These "zoo schools" have grown in number over the past few decades and have a high success rate in placing their graduates in zoos as interns and full-time employees. The competition to get into these schools, however, is intense. Some students apply after earning a bachelor's degree at a four-year college. Others transfer to a four-year school after getting their associate degree at the zoo college.

One of the oldest and most successful of these teaching zoo programs is the Exotic Animal Training and Management Program (EATM) at Moorpark College in Moorpark, California. Graduates earn Animal Science degrees and certificates in Animal Training and Wildlife Education. Many Moorpark graduates have gone on to successful careers at the San Diego

Zoo, the Los Angeles Zoo, and major Hollywood studios that have animal training departments.

After finishing their schooling, either from a four-year college or a two-year zoo program, graduates will enter a highly competitive job market. Some are lucky enough to immediately get positions interning at a zoo, aquarium, or other animal-care facility. The internship often leads to full-time zoo keeping jobs. Others may not find full-time work immediately and will continue to do volunteer or part-time work in the animal-care industry while pursuing a full-time keeper position.

Because the competition is so tough and there are limited openings in zoos, you should be willing to travel outside your state, or even your geographic region, to pursue job leads. The important

A student from the Exotic Animal Training and Management program of Moorpark College, California, teaches "Quinnie" to touch an object at Western PA Humane Society.

thing is to be persistent and stay positive. As one Moorpark graduate Kellie Snively puts it, "I don't think you can get a job in this industry unless you show it's something you really, really want to do."

The Classroom is a Zoo

The Moorpark Teaching Zoo was founded in 1974 by a former Moorpark College teacher, who also worked as a dolphin trainer for the United States Navy. Students work up to 70 hours a week feeding and caring for the more than 150 animals in the 5-acre zoo. On weekends the students run shows and animal demonstrations for the public, and each year plan an open house that attracts thousands of visitors.

"This place instills a really good work ethic," said graduate Jessica Forrest, who went on to a job at the San Diego Zoo. "They fully prepare you to work outside. They make sure you are ready."

Employers are equally impressed by Moorpark graduates. "The training the Moorpark students have had in doing public presentations and providing exotic animal care frequently makes them the most qualified hires we can get," said Jane Gilbert, animal training manager at the San Diego Zoo. "It's a wonderful fit for us and gives them good experience."

(Top) Frankie Giesseman, age 6, of Simi Valley, watches Clarence, a Galapagos tortoise who is 76 years old and weighs 575 pounds (260 kg) at America's Teaching Zoo at Moorpark College in Moorpark, California.

(Opposite) Clarence gets some attention from a student at America's Teaching Zoo at Moorpark College as visitors at the zoo look on.

THREE

Zookeepers at Work

According to the American Association of Zoo Keepers (AAZK), a national organization, there are more than 3,000 zookeepers working at 250 animal-care facilities across the United States. These include zoos, aquariums, wildlife parks, animal preserves, and animal rehabilitation centers. What do all these keepers do? A zookeeper's basic responsibility is to help take care of his or her animals' physical and mental health. But they do this in many different ways. You can get a better idea of all the things zookeepers do by following them through a typical day.

A Day in the Life

Upon arriving at the zoo, the keeper starts the workday looking over the redbooks. These are the daily journals that contain important summaries of what has been going on in the keeper's area, whether it is with exotic birds, familiar mammals, or scaly reptiles. The keeper reviews the redbook to get an overview of the particular section of the zoo. This helps the keeper know what to look for, or expect from, the animals in the day ahead.

(Opposite) A friendly llama looks over the shoulder of zookeeper Angela Ryan as she makes notes on the llamas in her care during ZSL London Zoo's annual stocktake.

The American Association of Zoo Keepers

The American Association of Zoo Keepers (AAZK) was formed in 1967 at the San Diego Zoo by several zookeepers who wanted to create an organization to promote professionalism in their job. According to the group's website, it is dedicated to "advancing animal care, promoting public awareness, enhancing professional development, and contributing to local and global conservation through fund-raising and stewardship." The AAZK currently has more than 2,800 members in 48 states, 5 Canadian provinces, and 24 other countries. The organization sponsors workshops, newsletters, Internet forums, and an annual conference held in a different city each September. In 2014, the conference will take place in Orlando, Florida, and in 2015, in St. Louis, Missouri. The AAZK uses these various venues to disseminate information that will help zookeepers "stay current in husbandry, training, nutrition, and conservation." The organization's national headquarters are in Topeka, Kansas.

(Above) Zookeeper Thomas Warkentin carries Saskia, a Burmese python who is 10 feet (3 m) long.

(Opposite) A coati enjoys honey given to it by a zookeeper at the Israeli zoo of Ramat Gan, north of the Mediterranean coastal city of Tel Aviv.

A zookeeper tickles a hippo's tongue at the Erlebniswelt zoo in Westphalia, Germany.

(Opposite) Keeper Sri Wahyuningsih feeds a 26-day-old endangered Sumatran tiger cub at the Taman Safari Indonesia Animal Hospital in West Java, Indonesia.

Next it's time to walk through the area. Making the rounds to the cages and enclosures for the animals, the keeper makes sure each creature is present and where it should be. The keeper looks for other things, too, such as each animal's physical appearance and behavior. Does it look healthy? Are there any signs of illness or injury? Is the animal eating properly?

Now it's mealtime. Food is brought in daily and stored in the zoo kitchen. Each animal has its own special diet, determined by the zoo **nutritionist**. It is the keeper's job to weigh the proper amount of food, prepare it the way the animals likes it (chopping, grinding, cooking) and then bring it to the enclosures. After the animals have eaten and **defecated**, it's time to clean up. Urine is hosed

down and fecal matter raked, but not before the keeper examines it carefully for any signs of a change in digestion or illness. Fecal samples are routinely collected and brought to the medical lab where they are examined and analyzed. The entire enclosure is cleaned, as well as the back areas that the public doesn't see: where the animal rests and sleeps. If an animal is found to be sick, it is the keeper's job to assist the zoo **veterinarian** in the examination process, and with administering medicine. It may mean wrapping ill-tasting or bad-smelling medicine in the animal's favorite food so it will eat it. Or it may mean keeping the animal calm and still while the vet gives it a shot or **vaccine**.

A Chinese animal trainer trains tigers and lions at a zoo in Fuzhou, in southeast China's Fujian province.

Training and Enrichment

At some time in the busy day, when the routine chores are done, the keeper works with animals in training and enrichment. This is a period all keepers look forward to because it provides them with quality, one-on-one time with each animal. Just like you teach your pet dog to follow certain commands, the keeper does so with these more exotic animals. Using treats as rewards, the keeper trains the animal to follow simple commands that are important to caring for it. For example, the keeper might train it to open its mouth in order to examine its teeth, or to step onto a scale to record its weight. If the keeper gives lectures or demonstrations to the public, he might train the animal to do more complicated things, like retrieve an object, roll over, or perform tricks.

Enrichment is more challenging for both keeper and animal. It is playtime with a purpose. The keeper devises activities meant to stimulate the animal's physical and mental abilities and keep it interested in its environment. It may mean hiding food and seeing if the animal can find it using its sense of smell. It might be getting the animal to manipulate a feeder to release food. Without such stimulation, zoo animals can lose interest, grow depressed, or even become physically ill.

There are other things to do, depending on the individual keeper. If he or she is part of the educational department, the keeper on any given day may lead guests on a zoo tour, give a lecture, or lead an animal presentation or demonstration. If the keeper is interested and has expertise in breeding or research programs, part of his or her day will be devoted to working in these areas.

The zookeeper's day ends as it began, with paperwork. The keeper writes up a detailed daily report on its charges, which will be read by management, including senior keepers and curators. It is important that all information about the animal be recorded clearly so supervisors know the condition of every animal.

It's a long day, and now it's time to go home and get some rest. Every day in the life of a zookeeper is a combination of daily routine and unexpected challenges and surprises.

How Much Can You Make?

Salaries for zookeepers are among the lowest in the animal care professions. The salary range in 2013 was $16,524 to $40,381, with a median income of $26,662. Starting salaries vary according to previous experience, education level, and the geographic region. Graduates of Santa Fe Community College's zoo program make an average starting salary of $20,000 to $23,000 as zookeepers. The Moorpark program in California quotes starting salaries of $23,000 to $28,000. Even though the pay is not high, getting a zoo keeping position is highly competitive. The work offers unique opportunities for young people who want to work in zoos and existing positions are limited. Some keepers work their way up to more senior positions, such as supervisors and managers, where the salaries can be considerably higher.

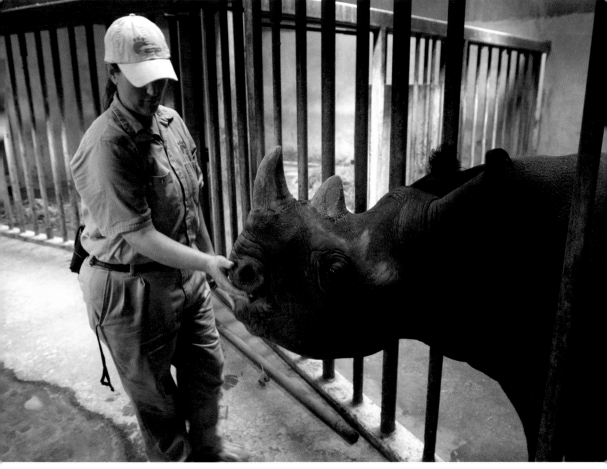

(Above) A zookeeper feeds a hungry rhino at the Sedgwick County Zoo in Wichita, Kansas.

(Opposite) A zookeeper brushes Beau, a 6-year-old Masi giraffe, in the Franklin Park Zoo's giraffe holding area. Three months ago the keepers could not even touch Beau, who they have been training to be more comfortable around people.

FOUR

Explore Your Options

Getting a position as a zookeeper is not easy. Competition is high, and available openings are limited. Once a person lands a job, however, there are some possible options ahead for the new keeper.

Specializing

A junior keeper will need to be flexible and may begin his or her career working in a number of different areas or sections of a zoo. However, when the opportunity arises to work with one species or group of animals, the new keeper should take advantage of it. Specialization is key to a successful career as a zookeeper. Keepers who specialize in one species or animal group become experts in an area over time. This makes them a valuable resource. Eventually, the keeper could be promoted to senior or head keeper in that section, overseeing the work of the other keepers.

Of course, there are other areas of specialization that can be just as rewarding. One of the main purposes of zoos, especially large ones, is to breed species to **propagate** and increase their numbers. This is especially true of animals that are considered **endangered species**. Successful breeding can result in more animals to be shared with other zoos, or even released back into the

(Opposite) A one-day-old mhorr gazelle is fed by a zookeeper at a zoo in Hungary.

wild. Keepers can be part of the breeding program, helping in the reproductive procedures and later nurturing the new babies that are produced.

Another option open to keepers in specialized animal care is working in a zoo hospital. Working under highly trained zoo veterinarians, keepers offer needed assistance for animal patients who are sick or injured, or new animals

(Right) A keeper tells young visitors about a tortoise in a zoo's educational department.

(Opposite) Zoo staff members show baby twin pandas at Adventure World in Shirahama, Wakayama, Japan.

sent from other zoos that need to be medically evaluated. The hospital is an area that demands great skill to work in, and requires physical stamina as well as a good working knowledge of many different animals and medical procedures.

Working with the Public

Although a keeper's main job is working with animals, he or she must also be able to work with people. Answering visitors' questions about the animals and making their visit pleasant is also part of the job. A keeper with good people skills who is adept at public speaking may consider becoming part of the zoo's educational wing—leading zoo tours, giving lectures, and performing animal presentations and demonstrations for the public. It's an important role that not only educates and entertains, but also reminds

A San Diego Zoo employee with a harpy eagle.

visitors of the importance of animal life and its preservation in our world today.

Other Options

There are other kinds of zoo work that may appeal to you other than being an animal keeper. If you like to cook and work with food, you might want to become a zoo cook or kitchen worker. They prepare meals for the various animals daily. In some large zoos that might mean feeding thousands of animals.

Zoo police officers play an important role in zoos. They are specially trained to make sure visitors don't deliberately or accidentally harm the animals and, in turn, make sure the visitors aren't harmed by the animals. They also answer questions, give directions, and provide any assistance a zoo visitor may need.

Zoos also employ artists and builders who plan and design new zoo exhibits. They try to create exhibits that will make the animals feel as at home as if they were in their natural environment. Artists also illustrate and write placards that give visitors information about the animals and their behavior.

From Keeper to Manager

Some keepers' interests lie in another direction. They find over time that they have a gift for supervising and management. Each main area of the

Doctor Zookeeper

Andrew Lentini has one of the more interesting and satisfying zoo keeping jobs. He is keeper in charge of amphibians and reptiles at the Toronto Zoo's Animal Health Center. He helps care for sick, injured, or stressed animals as well as new arrivals that need to

be medically examined before entering the zoo population. "Helping these animals settle in, start feeling and get better are my favorite parts of my job," he says.

Doing this is not easy when your patient is a massasauga rattlesnake, the Province of Ontario's only **venomous** snake, or an African dwarf crocodile. Lentini doesn't mind working with the snakes, which are his favorite animal, but the tiny crocodiles can present problems. Before attempting to handle them, he covers their eyes to keep them calm and secures their jaws so they can't bite. He also uses special tools to control their movements.

Like any hospital, there are successes and failures. "Despite our best efforts, sometimes we cannot help these animals and they die or we have to put them to sleep," Lentini says. "Those are the worst days for me."

Karen Killmar, associate curator of mammals at the San Diego Zoo, points to Allen's swamp monkeys in their enclosure. Killman helped rescue four of these monkeys from illegal sellers in Africa's Congo.

zoo has its own curator, a person who oversees all animals and employees in that section. Curators have less time working directly with the animals and spend more time at a desk doing paperwork. There are advantages to the job, other than more regular hours and better pay. Curators represent the zoo at **forums** and conferences and get to travel to other zoos to see what they're doing. They also help develop zoo policy and programs. "Keeping track of population statistics, breeding programs, and conservation fieldwork is all part of our job, and those areas are dynamic and ever-changing," says Karen Killmar, associate curator of mammals at the San Diego Zoo. "The job is never boring."

Zookeeper Rene Hinte holds a young tiger at the zoo in Magdeburg, Germany.

An animal keeper stands next to a tapir and its baby, who was born less than a month ago, at the zoo in Lille, France.

Whatever option a person chooses in the world of zoo keeping, the work is always challenging and tremendously satisfying. "It is one of the very best things about my life," says Amy Alfredy, a senior keeper at the San Diego Zoo's koala barn. "It really gives me a sense of purpose and personal satisfaction knowing that I am not only giving my best care to these amazing animals but am directly involved in helping them in their natural habitats."

A koala bear eats eucalyptus leaves, its only food, while clinging to the tree's trunk at the San Diego Zoo.

FIVE

Meet the Zookeepers

Rick Schwartz considers himself a lucky guy. He is doing what he always dreamed of doing since he first visited the San Diego Zoo on a family vacation in junior high school. He is a zookeeper in their Children's Zoo, where he and the other keepers take care of thirty animals. Rick's workday starts at 6 a.m. when he arrives to feed the animals.

"The coolest part of my job is whenever an animal that I know greets me and is happy to see me. … Any pet owner knows that's one of the best feelings. I get that every day just showing up to work."

After feeding, Rick's day consists of cleaning the enclosures, checking on each animal, meeting with staff, and greeting and answering the questions of hundreds of children and parents who visit the Children's Zoo each day.

Rick's dream job didn't happen right away. It took years of hard work and persistence to get there. After graduating from the Moorpark College zoo program, he got a job training birds, dogs, and cats for television and movies. Subsequent jobs included working with 150 birds at a hotel in Las Vegas and training guide dogs for blind people in Oregon. He applied six times to be a zookeeper at the San Diego Zoo and never even got an interview. Finally, he got a part-time keeper job there and six months later was hired full time.

(Opposite) Keeper Andreas Doerflein goes nose to nose with Knut, a 6-month-old polar bear, at the Berlin Zoo in Germany.

A young child reaches out from her father's shoulders to feed a giraffe.

When he's not working at the Children's Zoo, Rick is a Zoo Ambassador. In that role he leads community talks about animals and conservation, and appears with zoo animals on television and radio programs. Recently, he traveled to Botswana in Africa to assist zoo conservation researchers in their tracking of elephants. Rick helped spread the word of the program by taking photos, working on videos, and writing an Internet **blog**.

"The key thing to remember is it's our job as humans to be good stewards of the planet," Rick says. "But what's really important is to realize that everything is connected. Just because we may not see it, we may not know the important job that a particular animal may have in the rest of the **ecosystem**. It's up to us to learn what that is and protect it."

Three one-month-old lioness cubs are held by a keeper as they take their first outing at the Ramat Gan Safari Park near Tel Aviv, Israel.

Celebrating Zookeepers

The third week of July is a special time for zookeepers across the country. It is National Zoo Keeper Week, first officially recognized in 2007 when two Congresswomen from California and Kansas brought the proposed resolution before Congress. The week is celebrated with dedication shows, special luncheons, and educational programs and seminars for visitors at 250 animal-related facilities across North America. The San Diego Zoo sponsors one of the most memorable Zoo Keeper Week annual events. Zookeepers and some of their favorite animal friends make an appearance on the ball field in a special ceremony before a San Diego Padres baseball game.

The King of the Jungle surveys his zoo domain.

Working with the Big Cats

Nearly three-quarters of all zookeepers today are women, and they work with every kind of zoo animal. Heather Vetter has been primary cat keeper at the Phoenix Zoo in Arizona for ten years. She works a ten-hour day and loves feeding and caring for the zoo's biggest **carnivores**, including two Sumatran tigers. "I'm not scared," she says, "but when I first started working with them, it was intimidating to have a large **predator** just inches away from you!"

Through a practice of "protective contact," Heather is always separated from the animals by a barrier. After placing their food in their living quarters, called a "night house," she locks them inside. "I can then go out into the exhibit and do what I need to do. Once I have finished my duties in the exhibit, I can then let them out."

Vetter says that she enjoys being "up close and personal with animals on a daily basis." Some of her most memorable moments with them are humorous. "One day, I was watching the female lioness sleeping on her back next to the pond that is in her exhibit," she recalls. "I could tell she was dreaming, and then she became so startled that she rolled right into the pond! Lions don't typically like the water, so it was quite a surprise for her. She hasn't slept that close to the pond since!"

Margaret, a 10-day-old giraffe, is bottle fed by Zookeeper Tim Rowlands in Chester, England. Margaret is the first Rothschild giraffe born at the zoo and is being hand reared after having difficulty suckling from her mother.

Feeding the Animals

While nutrition is a concern at every zoo, there are only 15 full-time zoo nutritionists in the United States. Two of them work at the San Diego Zoo and Safari Park—Jennifer Parsons and Michele Gaffney. Together they are responsible for the proper feeding of about 8,000 zoo animals. "I love figuring out riddles. Every day there is something new to solve and learn here," says Parsons. "This job is never boring!" The nutritionist's job includes making sure animals get the right diet of balanced foods, stay at their correct weight, and get their dietary needs met when they are pregnant, very young, or old. Diets are adjusted according to the season. Most animals, like humans, tend to eat more in the winter than the rest of the year.

"We are always evaluating nutritional food items and the health of the animals," says Gaffney, while admitting sometimes getting the animals to eat what's good for them can be a challenge. "We can put the best diet together for a species, but if they don't eat it, obviously it won't be nutritionally balanced for the animal."

SIX

What's Next?

In 2006, according to the American Association of Zoo Keepers, American zoos and aquariums were visited by 142 million people. That's more people than attendees at all professional football, baseball, and basketball games combined in the same period of time.

In the years to come, zoos will continue to play an important role in our society and cultural life. While television nature programs and live Internet cameras can bring wildlife closer than ever, nothing can replace the thrill of being a few inches away from an exotic monkey, bird, or big cat in real life, an experience only a zoo can provide.

The outlook for zoo keeping as a profession isn't especially good. Other careers in the animal care and service industry are expected to grow through 2018, outpacing many other professions, but keepers will not. Why is this happening? For one, the number of zoos is low and not expected to grow, and the job market for keepers will remain limited. As a result, the competition for these positions, when they open, is fierce. Despite relatively low pay and long hours, people who want to work at zoos are passionate about this important work.

(Opposite) This cute baby koala gets plenty of attention from its keeper.

A giant panda is being examined by its keeper at the Research and Breeding Center, Chengdu, Sichuan, China.

Comfort and Safety

The future of zoos will depend largely on reliable, creative, and hardworking zookeepers. They can make a difference in many of the challenges facing zoos today, as well as in the future. Although zoos have made great strides in creating natural environments where animals feel at home, there is still work to be done. Many animals remain in restrictive and outdated enclosures that diminish their lives. Zookeepers who see and work with animals in these problematic settings can be the best advocates for change and better living conditions.

Zoo animals face difficulties, and so do the keepers who care for them. Safety is a critical issue for zookeepers. An average of ten keepers die from fatal injuries caused by animals each year. Many of these fatalities occur at unaccredited animal centers, but some take place at prestigious zoos. Written safety programs need to be developed at every zoo and followed by all zoo workers. Safety training for keepers is a necessity, and the best preventive measures need to be put in place. Zoos need to be more thoughtful of their keepers and not overwork them. When a keeper is tired or rushed, mistakes are made and accidents can happen.

A lowland gorilla watches the crowd of visitors gathered to see him.

Where Animals Run Free

Animal parks are an alternative to traditional zoos, where animals are viewed in cages and other enclosures. In a wild animal park, the animals roam freely in an environment meant to duplicate their natural one, wherever that may be. The people are the ones behind barriers, such as enclosed trams that travel through the park, allowing them to see the animals much as they might in the wild.

The largest and most celebrated wild animal park in the United States is the San Diego Zoo's Safari Park, formerly called the Wild Animal Park. Opened in 1972, the Safari Park lies 32 miles (52 km) from the San Diego Zoo near Escondido, California, and covers 1,800 acres. More than 2,600 animals, representing more than 300 species from six continents, inhabit the park. The park contains replicas of African plains and a **savanna**, a gorilla forest, an elephant valley, and the replica of a village in Nairobi, Kenya. About two million people visit the Safari Park each year viewing animals from trams, guided carts, and even a zip line that stretches nearly a mile.

Breeding Programs and Conservation

A lot of attention has been placed in recent years on training and enrichment for zookeepers. There has been less emphasis on an equally important area of zoo work: breeding programs. By assisting endangered animals in the reproduction process, zoos ensure these species will not disappear from the face of the earth, even if they have in the wild. With proper nurturing and training, some of these newborns may eventually be reintroduced back into their natural habitats.

A newborn Francois' Langur monkey is fed by its keeper at the London Zoo.

Reproductive programs are part of the larger issue of the conservation of animals and the habitats in which they thrive. While directors and curators often fashion these conservation programs, keepers are the people who are the face of the zoo to the general public. Through educational programs, lectures, demonstrations, and workshops, experienced and passionate keepers can spread the word. They can raise the public's consciousness of the importance of saving all kinds of animals for Earth's future.

Zoos play an important role in the lives of both humans and animals. And dedicated, hardworking, caring zookeepers have been key to the success of zoos in the past and present, and will continue to be so in the future.

This cheetah cub has a new home at the Smithsonian's National Zoo in Washington, D.C., and is being raised by humans.

Breeding Cheetahs

Zoos currently breed about 160 endangered species in captivity. By doing so, they hope to raise enough animals in zoos to guarantee the survival of the species when the animals die out in the wild. But many of these animals are difficult to breed in zoos. A good example is the cheetah, which is not endangered yet, but losing population rapidly. Over the past two decades, of 281 cheetahs in North American zoos, only 15 cubs have been born in an average year despite great efforts and expensive breeding programs. When it comes to mating, cheetahs are finicky and do not breed as easily as bigger wild cats, such as lions and tigers.

One answer to the cheetah problem is the Population Manager Center at Lincoln Park Zoo in Chicago. It carefully analyzes breeding methods at 235 zoos nationwide and then recommends how to best breed each species. It recommends conservation centers for certain animals hard to breed, including the cheetah. These centers are like wild animal parks with wide, open spaces that may make the cheetah feel more at home and less stressed than in a zoo environment. There are today five such centers for breeding cheetahs.

Glossary

accredited	certified, meeting necessary requirements
blog	a website on which an individual or group record opinions and information on a regular basis
carnivores	animals that eat the flesh of other animals
curator	a manager or supervisor of one section of a zoo or museum
defecate	passing voided solid body waste through the anus
ecology	branch of biology dealing with interrelations between animals and their environment
ecosystem	a system formed by the interaction of a community of animals and plants
enclosure	a contained area surrounded by a fence or other barrier where animals live and are exhibited in a zoo
endangered species	a species at risk of extinction (no longer existing)

forums	public meetings to discuss an issue or topic
habitat	the natural environment an animal lives in
herpetology	the branch of zoology that deals with reptiles and amphibians
menageries	small zoos that existed in Europe from the Middle Ages to the early 1800s
nutritionist	a trained expert in the dietary requirements of animals or people
predator	an animal that hunts other animals for food
propagate	to reproduce
savanna	a dry, grassy plain with some trees
species	a major category or group of animals that have certain traits in common
vaccine	a medicine made of weakened or killed bacteria that prevents disease
venomous	poisonous
veterinarian	a medical doctor who treats and cares for animals
zoology	the scientific study of animals

Find Out More

Books

Bowman, Debra D. *Today I think I'll Be... A Zookeeper*. Scotts Valley, CA: CreateSpace Independent Publishing Platform, 2010.

Curtis, Jennifer Keats. *Animal Helpers: Zoos*. Mount Pleasant, SC: Sylvan Dell Publishing, 2013.

Newman, Aline Alexander. *Ape Escapes! And More True Stories of Animals Behaving Badly*. Washington, DC: National Geographic Children's Books, 2012.

Treik, Sarah. *Zookeeper* (Big Buddy Book: Extreme Jobs). Minneapolis, MN: Big Buddy Books, 2011.

Websites

American Association of Zoo Keepers (AAZK)

www.aazk.org

Log on to learn about career opportunities as a zoo or aquarium keeper. Find information about activities and events, as well as links to other local chapters of AAZK.

Association of Zoos and Aquariums (AZA)

http://www.aza.org

The AZA is a nonprofit organization dedicated to the advancement of zoos and aquariums in the areas of conservation, education, science, and recreation. On its website you can view information on animal care and management and resources for careers in zoo and aquarium work.

The San Diego Zoo Website

www.sandiegozoo.org

The San Diego Zoo is the largest zoo in the United States. On its website you can learn about its many conservation projects and exhibits, and watch videos of various zoo animals.

Index

Page numbers in **boldface** are illustrations.

About the Author

Steven Otfinoski has written more than 150 books for young readers, including many about animals from koalas to scorpions. He lives in Connecticut with his wife, their daughter, and two dogs.